- Successful Dating -

No More Frogs
Scorpio

23 October – 21 November

by
Cathrine Dahl

CONTENTS

- Successful Dating -
No More Frogs

by Cathrine Dahl

No More Frogs - Successful Dating is your one-stop dating guide. No unnecessary blah-blah. The information is right here, at your fingertips.

This guide can be used in several ways. It's a handy tool when you want to prepare yourself a little. It can give you an advantage when going on a date or getting to know someone you've just met - or even someone you've known for a while.

Although this guide can help you angle your approach, remember to be true to yourself. Have fun, be wise, follow your heart - and keep your feet on the ground!

- Cathrine Dahl

Preface:
A few words about compatibility, and why compatibility guides can give you the wrong idea.

So you've met this Gemini you really, really like, but you're a Scorpio, and the compatibility guides say you're a lousy match. Guess what? That's rubbish!

Some compatibility guides offer a very simplistic approach, claiming that your best matches are the star signs within the same element as you:

Fire: Aries, Leo and Sagittarius
Earth: Taurus, Virgo and Capricorn
Air: Gemini, Libra and Aquarius
Water: Cancer, Scorpio and Pisces

Other guides are slightly more specific, declaring that we are compatible with star signs within our astrological polarity.

Yin: Taurus, Virgo, Capricorn, Cancer, Scorpio and Pisces
Yang: Aries, Leo, Sagittarius, Gemini, Libra and Aquarius

Doesn't look too good, does it? The most optimistic approach has removed half of the population from your dating pool. It doesn't make any sense. The true picture is far more promising...

One star sign, two very different personalities

Each of us has a unique astrological thumbprint determined by the sun, the moon and the planets. The most important factors being your ascending star (ascendant), the sun (star sign) and the moon (feelings).

Let's make it simple
Imagine your star sign being a melody. All the other aspects (the unique positioning of the moon and the planets) are sound effects, applied by a producer with a mixer.

The combination of rhythm, depth and base creates your unique sound. Another person with the same star sign will get his own sound mix and end up with a different beat.

Your personal melody can create wonderful harmonies with star signs you're not supposed to get on with – and nothing but noise with signs that are meant to be matches. You won't find out until you get to know each other.

Let's get to know your date...

THE MALE

YOUR DATE: SCORPIO
23 October–21 November

The Essence of him

Mysterious – sensual – intense – direct – reserved – charming – entertaining – interesting and knowledgeable – strongly influenced by his surroundings – cultivated and philosophical – suspicious – a good judge of character – needs control – kind – considerate – protective and loyal – sensitive – vindictive – supportive – has a good memory – creative – jealous

...and remember: Although this man is direct and to the point, he will wait until he knows you really well to open up about his feelings and who he is, deep down.

Blind Date – speedy essentials

Who's waiting for you?

It's the guy who looks at you as you enter the room. Yes, he will be smiling, but that's not what gets you. The intensity of his gaze ... it's impossible to ignore. It will either make you a little nervous or very attracted, or both. All of this will happen quickly, even before he's had a chance to say hi. There's something magnetic and mysterious about him, something you can't put your finger on. This is what makes him so fascinating. He's an enigma, waiting to be explored and discovered. But be yourself. This man is a good judge of character and will notice if you try to fool him.

Emergency fixes for embarrassing pauses

Chances are slim that a Scorpio man will ever run out of things to talk about – but that doesn't mean there won't be a pause or two. This man communicates with his eyes. What you may interpret as an embarrassing pause may actually be a flirtation or a suggestion – or an erotic invitation. If you can handle this, you can handle a date with Mr Scorpio.

Your place or mine?

Love is not an important ingredient in this man's sex life. He's very passionate, and if he likes you, it won't be long before the casual conversation moves to the next level. The foreplay can actually start before you leave the restaurant. Weird? Not with this guy. He is a master of seduction. If you allow yourself to sink into his eyes, you may discover this yourself...

Checklist, before you dash out to meet him:

No heavy eye makeup
(hint: communicate with your yes)
Put your phone on silent
(hint: no guys calling you!)
Wear seductive underwear
(hint: you will radiate sensuality)
Wear a sassy and feminine outfit
(hint: nothing tacky)
Smile and make your voice lively
(hint: make him laugh and feel happy)

Tip: *Never* give the impression that you're interested in something without seeing it through, especially not when it comes to sex. You don't play around with this guy. A yes is a yes!

CHAPTER 1

PREPARE YOURSELF

Catch his eye, capture his attention
Top 10 attention grabbers

1. Be sparkling; make him laugh.
2. Be direct without being blunt.
3. Show attentiveness and affection.
4. Play along with his ideas and offer constructive opinions.
5. Wear something that will emphasise your curves.
6. Suggest new and interesting places to go: a small restaurant, an intimate club, etc.
7. Don't make yourself too accessible. He loves a challenge.
8. Make sure you have something interesting to tell him. Pay attention to details.
9. Use your eyes to communicate, and be sensual about it.
10. Be outgoing and social.

The SHE. The woman!

The Scorpio man wants a little bit of everything. It can be difficult to figure out which qualities make the 'must have' list. He is a passionate guy, and he seeks the same passion in his woman. She must be attractive and sexy. It's also important that she's intelligent, loyal and supportive. But without chemistry, communication will be difficult. If there's no chemistry, there's no future.

The Essence of her

Cheerful – erotic – flexible – sharp, with an independent mind – has a positive attitude and a constructive outlook– loyal – supportive – genuine – sexy, both in mind and appearance – liberated– faithful – passionate in bed – sensual and erotically playful – optimistic – feminine – assertive without being aggressive – attentive and admiring

Scorpio arousal meter
From 0 to 100... In an instant! A calm and laid-back Scorpio can transform himself into a passionate dream very quickly. Be prepared.

Remember: Be true to yourself

It doesn't matter if he is the most stunning guy you've ever met – if you don't match, you don't match. You may be able to put on a show for a while to hold his attention, but what's the point? We can't please everybody. We all have different needs, dreams, tastes and preferences. There's no such thing as a one-size-fits-all lover. Be yourself, and be true to who you are – always!

Very important: He can read your mood, body language and expressions. Don't try to hide anything from him. Got something on your mind? Let it out.

CHAPTER 2

THE FIRST DATE

Getting your foot in the door
The basics

A touch of mystery. He loves a challenge, so don't make yourself too accessible. This doesn't mean you should play hard to get, but resist throwing yourself at him. Show interest, but keep a slight distance.

Joy! He loves women who can make him laugh and bring out the bright side of life, so make sure to show him your sparkling and playful side.

Easy on the jokes. Take him seriously. Making jokes on his behalf, no matter how innocently, is a no-no! It will turn him off you completely.

He'll call your bluff. He observes, analyses and interprets body language with great ease. If you put on a show, he will call your bluff. Never try to impress him by being someone you're not – anyway, why would you?

Be flexible - and genuine! Keep an open mind. Be flexible. Stubborn discussions give him a headache. Be genuine. If you pay him a compliment, make sure you mean it.

Whatever you do...

- **DON'T** flirt with other men (!).

- **DON'T** signal that you're erotically interested if you're not.

- **DON'T** dismiss his ideas. Take him seriously.

- **DON'T** provoke him or start an argument unnecessarily.

- **DON'T** be too critical

Remember, he can spot a fake quickly. Be open. Be genuine. Be yourself.

- **DON'T** be shy. Return his direct glance.

- **DON'T** be negative in your views of the world.

- **DON'T** dress too conservatively.

- **DON'T** ignore him and start talking to others.

- **DON'T** betray his trust.

He is very supportive,
provided you play it straight.

Signs you're in - or not

The Scorpio is a passionate man, and he's either in or he's out. If he likes you, he will let you know – but in his own way. When it comes to showing feelings and romantic interest, he prefers nonverbal communication or actions. Words tend to get a little awkward for him. If you are on the same level and able to read each other by observing, this won't be a problem. However, if you're not familiar with his style of communicating, the following signs may indicate that he's got his eyes on you:

Chances are he will...

- call you the same evening
- be supportive of your ideas
- organise something for you to do together, maybe a trip
- treat you to coffee or dinners
- be focused on you and won't notice other women in the room
- be eager to be physically close to you

Not your type? Making an exit

Don't worry – a relationship with a Scorpio will seldom come to the point of needing to stage an escape. Although he bonds quickly with someone who sparks his romantic interest, he disappears just as abruptly if things aren't working out. Sure, he may slam a few doors, wave his arms around and raise his voice, but that's about it – and then he'll be gone. Minimally, he needs a woman who he can relate to, who's supportive and who can make his days pleasant and passionate. Why would he waste time on someone who can't provide the basics?

However, some unusual Scorpio men may become stuck in a fantasy. They fail to grasp reality and reach for a dream that faded ages ago. In this case, you don't have much choice but to be blunt about it. Prepare yourself. There will be passionate arguments – but he will eventually realise that a more rewarding relationship awaits him elsewhere.

Foolproof exit measures:

These tips are far from nice. However, if you really want to send him a message, any of the following will do the trick.

- Tell him you're not in the mood for sex and that he can go ahead and please himself without you
- When you do have sex, complain about his lovemaking and insist on doing things your way
- Flirt with other men whenever you're out together
- Pursue your own interests alone in the evenings
- Joke around whenever he wants to have a serious conversation
- Be stubborn and inflexible. Turn every little gripe into a major discussion

CHAPTER 3

SEX'N STUFF

Seductive moves:
How to get him in the mood:

He is an adventurous guy who is open to suggestions. Teasing can make him go wild, but don't confuse this with playing hard to get. Pretending not to be interested – if you are – is a turn-off. If she does things right, a woman who is playful and sensual can bring out his passion. Stripping is a great example of this, especially if you don't allow him to touch you.

Preferences and erotic nature

A Scorpio man wants to dazzle you, surprise you, please you and dominate you, all at the same time – and he usually succeeds. He knows exactly what to do and will probably discover erogenous zones you never knew you had. Soft cuddles and sweet kisses won't do it for him. He feeds on passion and intensity, and he wants you to come on strong – but without being aggressive. He doesn't mind using sexual gadgets in order to explore sensations and satisfy his partner and himself. But don't make the mistake of thinking he doesn't know what to do with his hands. He's an expert!

Hitting the right buttons

Although every sign has areas that are more sensitive than others, individual sensitivity may vary quite a bit. Don't go body-blind. Honing in on these erogenous zones and forgetting the rest of him is not a good idea. Use his erogenous zones to create sparks while turning him on, and as a passion booster when it gets heated. Watch his body language – including the most obvious of signs! Open your mind to the sensuality of touch and taste.

Key areas
His genitals

Get it on

All things erotic combine in this man: he loves women, he loves the chase – provided it doesn't go on for ever – and he loves sex. And his erogenous zone? His genitals! No matter how complicated he may seem, pleasing him is simple and straightforward.

Arouse him

Star signs with less obvious erogenous zones are easier to arouse in public – it can be as simple as touching their hands, back or legs. Not so with Mr Scorpio. Casually stimulating his genitals in a public place requires creativity. Crowded rooms and tightly packed queues could provide a chance to get close to him. You could always ask to feel the fabric of his trousers... But remember, as soon as he's aroused, he will not be easily contained. Don't fool around with this guy!

Surprise him

A big turn-on for this man is a woman who can undress him with her eyes in a public place. If the sexual chemistry between you is strong, it won't take long before he starts getting hot ... start practising!

Spice it up

Scorpio is a water sign, which means he loves showering with you – and rubbing his body against yours while you're at it. Oils and creams usually produce positive results. Be creative.

Remember: Never start something you don't intend to finish. As soon as you have turned him on, there will be no looking back.

His expectations

Lots of tenderness. His ideal partner is warm, tender and passionate.

Running the show. He's not too keen on sexually aggressive women. Playing second fiddle is not his style. However, a passive partner is even worse – he finds it boring.

Don't be shy, be loud.   His partner must show interest, take the initiative and clearly display how she feels – preferably in a physical way.

Erotic enigmas. He loves when his partner provides with the erotic inspiration that allows him to explore the mysteries of sex even further.

Feeling free. Sexual chemistry is very important to him. His partner needs to be on the same level in order for him to feel truly liberated and uninhibited.

There is a time and place... Careful playfulness can be a great kick, provided it happens before things get too hot and steamy.

Embrace passion. The most important things of all is that his partner must clearly show appreciation for his intense passion.

Your sensual preferences
Quiz yourself and find out whether this man is for you.

Where on the scale are you?
1 = Don't agree | 3 = Sure | 5 = Agree!

1. Sex without intense passion and intensity is not worth having.
One a scale for 1 to 5, you are: 1 - 2 - 3- 4 - 5

2. Too much sensitivity and gentle kissing can ruin the passion.
One a scale for 1 to 5, you are: 1 - 2 - 3- 4 - 5

3. A strong and dominating partner makes it easier to display passion in bed.
One a scale for 1 to 5, you are: 1 - 2 - 3- 4 - 5

4. New positions and gadgets are important for keeping a sex life satisfying.
One a scale for 1 to 5, you are: 1 - 2 - 3- 4 - 5

Score 15–20: Fierce – intense – passionate – satisfying – 100% wow.
10 - 14: This man can bring you to new heights and make you feel amazing. Sometimes, you may need to make an effort to keep up with him.
5 - 9: He'll sweep you off your feet in no time, but things may become a little too intense in the long run. Talk to him. He wants to please you, so he will adjust.
1 - 4: Be prepared: this is a passionate guy. He could open new erotic doors for you – or, if you're not into it, shut down the erotic vibes completely.

CHAPTER 4

GENERAL STUFF

The big picture

Keep in mind that the characteristics of a Scorpio may vary quite a bit depending on where within the sign he was born, as well as a wide range of additional astrological factors. But for now, let's stick to the basics. Just remember: don't jump to conclusions as soon as you meet him. Give him room to shine. Get to know the man behind the sign.

His personality: Pros and cons

Pros	Cons
• Mysterious and sensual	• Jealous
• Intense and direct	• Stubborn
• Persistent	• Domineering
• Creative	• Temperamental
• Energetic	• Reserved
• Passionate	• Suspicious
• Sensitive	• Controlling
• An excellent observer	• Evasive
• Knowledgeable	• Vindictive
• A good judge of character	• Secretive
• Kind and considerate	• Ruthless
• Protective and loyal	• Arrogant
• Courageous	• Possessive
• Thorough	• Unforgiving

Tip: How to show romantic interest

Be direct. Show interest in him – not only as a man, but as a person with an interesting life. Be supportive and affectionate. Let him know he can trust you.

Romantic Vibes

Mr Scorpio:
The protective and loyal partner

The essence

Love is everything. When this man falls in love, he falls deeply. Superficial flings and casual romantic affairs do not exist in his world. Love absorbs him, and he feels it intensely.

...and love is never a chore! Although he bonds easily with a woman who has captured his heart, she should never take him, nor his feelings, for granted. This man does not waste his time.

Sparks might fly. Love and chemistry are the essence of his relationships, which require constant nourishment in order to grow.

A bumpy ride. He is no easy partner – in fact, he can be quite the challenge. Although he's kind and generous, he can also be jealous, temperamental and demanding.

Pick up the signals. Women who need vocal and direct affirmation will probably find his nonverbal approach a bit frustrating. His partner must be able to interpret his tone of voice, the way he looks at her and his body language.

Get close. He truly enjoys intimacy and privacy. A supersocial Scorpio may turn into a homebody when he finds the woman of his dreams.

Tip: How to show erotic interest

If you know how to communicate with him, showing erotic interest is easy. Allow your glance to linger on him, give him playful smiles and touch him gently with the tips of your fingers.

Erotic Vibrations

Mr Scorpio:
The intense and passionate lover

The essence

Keep the fire alive. If you long for regular, passionate, sexual encounters, this guy comes close to being the ultimate erotic dream.

Getting on top of things. Sometimes, he may come across as slightly dominating in bed. Don't be put off by this – it's just one of many ways that he gets his kicks.

Extensive menu. He can get into virtually anything, provided it gives you pleasure! In his attempts to please you, he may get slightly carried away at times. If this happens, just tell him to slow down a bit.

Take part, be active. Don't be fooled into thinking you can just lay back and enjoy the whole thing! A Scorpio man will expect you to play an active role. If you fail to do so, he will probably start wondering what's wrong, and he'll eventually lose interest.

Endurance. His energy seems to last for ever. This guy can go all night without tiring!

Imagination rules. Just when you think that the two of you have tried everything under the sun, Mr Scorpio will suggest something new and exciting.

CHAPTER 5

COMPATIBILITY QUIZ

Are you banging your head against the wall, or does he unleash your positive potential? Do you provoke him or bring out the best in him? Does he make you throw your arms up in exasperation, or do you feel inspired and complete in his company? Are the two of you headed towards doom or dream? Take the test to find out.

Question 1.
How do you deal with a jealous partner?

A. It annoys me. I wish my man would trust me more.
B. Even though it makes me roll my eyes, I actually find it flattering and reassuring. It's a way to know he cares.
C. I would never give him reason to be. Why would I flirt with other men when I have the world's greatest partner?

Question 2.
You're out having dinner with a guy you've just met. How do you respond when he starts gazing deeply into your eyes?

A. I'd probably get nervous and start playing with my napkin...
B. I'd ask him if he lost a contact lens.
C. I'd return his gaze with a sensual one of my own, and we'd take it from there...

(cont.)

Question 3.
Do you think it's possible to communicate without words?

A. How else are you supposed to communicate?!
B. Yes, absolutely. Sometimes, a glance can say more than a thousand words.
C. It depends on the situation. Words are occasionally necessary to avoid misunderstandings.

Question 4.
Do you enjoy flirting for its own sake?

A. No. I only flirt when I want to accomplish something.
B. Sometimes, but I never intend to hurt anybody.
C. Of course. It's game; everybody knows that. I enjoy sparking interest in men.

Question 5.
Do you tend to dish out comments and opinions without thinking?

A. Very seldom. I don't like getting hurt, so I'm careful to risk hurting others.
B. If criticism is called for, I'm blunt and direct about it. People need to be able to handle the truth.
C. Sometimes, but only if I'm angry.

Question 6.
What's your attitude to sex?

A. Sex? Sweaty and boring. I'm not into it, actually.
B. Although I enjoy sex, whether or not I'm up for it depends on my mood.
C. Sex and passion are essential in a relationship. Without them, it's just a friendship.

Question 7.
Do you need many people around you to thrive?

A. Not really – especially if I'm in a loving and passionate relationship.
B. It's not important, provided my partner and I get out and socialise from time to time.
C. I have an active social life and thrive with people around me. Spending time on my own makes me feel restless.

Question 8.
Are you stubborn in discussions with your partner?

A. Rarely. Flexibility usually produces more positive results.
B. Yes. My partner is stubborn, and it provokes me.
C. Sometimes, but only if the topic is really important to me.

Question 9.
Would you describe yourself as optimistic?

A. Most of the time, but I never lose sight of reality.
B. Yes. Being positive is a game-changer. You can achieve so much more.
C. Above all, I'm realistic. Then I can add optimism and enthusiasm, if it's appropriate.

Question 10.
What are your preferences in bed?

A. Soft, sensitive and romantic.
B. Creative, erotic and tender.
C. Hot, passionate and intense.

SCORE	A	B	C
Question 1	1	5	10
Question 2	5	1	10
Question 3	1	10	5
Question 4	10	5	1
Question 5	10	1	5
Question 6	1	5	10
Question 7	5	10	1
Question 8	10	1	5
Question 9	5	10	1
Question 10	1	5	10

75 – 100

Suddenly, there he was, pushing all of the competition aside. He dazzled you and swept you off your feet. You're probably still amazed by it. Life is never boring with him. He brings out the passion in you and makes you experience life in a completely different way; he makes you feel alive. It's almost as if he has kissed you out of a deep sleep, like in a fairy tale – a very passionate fairy tale. In return, you provide him with the love, support and reassurance he needs to feel safe and grounded. It's a good match. Enjoy each other!

51 – 74

The two of you have a unique way of communicating – it sometimes feels as if you can read each other's minds. But that doesn't mean you always agree. There might be a rumble of thunder from time to time, but a thunderstorm always leaves the air clear and refreshing. You are well aware that behind the macho exterior hides a sensitive boy, and you would never do anything to hurt him. In fact, you feel very protective towards him. He admires your calmness, patience and your ability to bring out the sunshine, no matter how grey the day. You also bring out the passion in him – and that's something you can both fully enjoy. There's excellent harmony here, and wonderful days ahead...

26 – 50

You're either extremely patient and flexible – or you are head over heels in love. The way things are now, you probably find yourself sacrificing to make things work. But how long are you prepared to do so? There are limits to everything. If you give too much and get little fulfillment in return, the warm feelings will eventually fade. You have two options: you can either tell him about your frustrations and give him a chance to adjust – or you can recognise that the man of your dreams is waiting somewhere else. But don't wait too long. Nothing will happen until you take the first step. The only question is whether to step into the relationship or out of it...

10 – 25

He is a mystery, an erotic challenge – and someone who provokes you endlessly. Is it curiosity that makes you stay, or are you doing it out of habit? Or, perhaps, are you waiting to teach him a lesson? This won't be productive. Staying for the wrong reasons will yield the wrong results. Isn't it time you committed to finding true love – and a sex life that brings you pleasure? You need someone different in your life, and he probably does too. Let it go. Move on with your life. Love, sensuality and happiness await you both elsewhere.

Thoughts...
Things may not always be as they seem. Don't rely on a quiz to give you big answers - talk to him and embrace the positive feelings.

THE FEMALE

YOUR DATE: SCORPIO
23 October–21 November

The Essence of her

Guarded of her feelings – sensual – warm, with a big heart – jealous – temperamental and moody – energetic – independent – passionate about everything she does – confident and determined – choosy – interested in people, but keeps a distance until she get to know them – has a strong personality – a perfectionist, both professionally and personally

...and remember: She may be blunt at times, but don't be put off by her sharp remarks or insensitive comments. They're not intended to hurt or upset you – unless she's angry!

Blind Date – speedy essentials

Who's waiting for you?

The Scorpio woman won't be waiting for you. She won't be early, but she'll make an entrance when she does arrive. She will expect you to admire her as she enters the room – so being late, even by two minutes, is not an option! If you are, you'll be in for an awkward start to the evening, and you may find yourself kicked out before long. This woman is worth being on time for: she has a deep sensuality about her, a feminine seductiveness that men find irresistible. She's probably very attractive – not necessarily because of what she's wearing, but because of who she is.

Emergency fixes for embarrassing pauses.

You'd better hope this isn't an issue, because too many pauses will be her cue to take off, and she'll do this with icy politeness. You are supposed to entertain her, dazzle her and make her feel admired. Pauses will make her feel uneasy – and there are no second chances. Make sure the conversation is flowing casually with stories about interesting things you've seen or experienced. Allow her to interact, and never try to control the conversation. Show genuine interest. Ask intelligent questions. Need to catch your breath and gather your thoughts for a minute? Order her a glass of champagne.

Your place or mine?

Either. A luxurious hotel room might work, too. The Scorpio woman is very choosy when it comes to men, but provided a guy lives up to her standards, she doesn't mind a little passionate fun. She has a healthy appetite for sex and is attracted to men with strong, masculine bodies. No crude comments. It takes a classy man to seduce this woman.

Checklist, before you dash out to meet her:

Wear clothing that emphasises your best features

(hint: don't overdo it – be classy)

Send a text to let her know she's on your mind

(hint: keep it short and alluring)

Have a snack before you meet up

(hint: don't suggest eating right away)

Have a little extra cash on you

(hint: in case you want to treat her to something special)

Keep your cell phone on on silent

(hint: no distractions)

Tip: She can be very stubborn. Never try to *tell* her anything. Constructive criticism must be disguised as praise and suggestions.

CHAPTER 1

PREPARE YOURSELF

Catch her eye, capture her attention
Top 10 attention grabbers

1. Maintain a relaxed and friendly attitude to the people around you.
2. Have a good sense of humour, with a warm and inviting laugh.
3. Be reserved with your attention. Don't throw yourself at her.
4. Buy her a little spontaneous gift.
5. Invite her for a drink – but make it champagne, not some cheap plonk.
6. Got a body worth showing off? Show it off! (But keep it classy and subtle).
7. Let her know that you're aiming high in life – but not building castles in the air.
8. Pay her intelligent compliments in public.
9. Ask for her opinion.
10. Have a nice car, an expensive watch … or something that indicates success.

The HE. The man!

He must be classy, strong and stylish. She needs a man she can look up to, respect and admire. Although she'd never admit it, she appreciates a steady guy who can keep her on track when her mood swings off course. Although she loves a strong body, it's love and loyalty that make the top of her list. Money and luxury is a plus, but if that's all he's got to show for himself, she'll be off.

The Essence of him
Masculine – funny, with a good sense of humour and a playful twinkle in his eyes – loyal – passionate, erotic and sensual – in control of his life, with a good job – generous; maybe even a bit extravagant at times – inspirational – understanding – intelligent – takes care of his body – attentive and admiring – reliable, no matter what

Scorpio arousal meter
From 0 to 100... At the speed of light, as long as you have connected with her and share a strong sexual chemistry

Remember: Be true to yourself

It doesn't matter if she is the most stunning girl you've ever met – if you don't match, you don't match. You may be able to put on a show for a while to hold her attention, but what's the point? We can't please everybody. We all have different needs, dreams, tastes and preferences. There's no such thing as a one-size-fits-all lover. Be yourself, and be true to who you are – always!

Very important: Don't let her run the show. If she seems bossy, it might be a test to see whether you're up to dating her. Take the initiative, be assertive and be prepared to display your masculine qualities.

CHAPTER 2

THE FIRST DATE

Getting your foot in the door
The basics

Be focused. Never glance at other women when courting her. She is jealous and won't tolerate a date who's a little too friendly with other women.

Take her seriously. Don't make fun of her opinions. You can question them – but only if you're intelligent about it and have something to offer.

...and be sincere! You won't charm her by throwing compliments around. She can tell the difference between a sincere compliment and a clever tactic to get into her bed.

Treat her. When inviting her out, don't be a cheapskate! Food trucks and fast food joints will be regarded as insults – unless you have something interested lined up afterwards.

Make it special. When courting a female Scorpio, you need to show her that you have made an effort to please her in some way – a romantic home cooked meal, for example.

Be attentive. Listen, ask questions and don't criticise. Pay attention to her: what she does, what she says – everything.

Whatever you do...

• **DON'T** flirt with – or even glance at – other women.

• **DON'T** take her interest for granted.

• **DON'T** be cheap. Pamper her.

• **DON'T** talk about previous girlfriends.

• **DON'T** criticise her views or tell her to do things differently.

Remember,
especially if you've just met, never take anything for granted. She won't keep a

- **DON'T** leave all the decisions to her.

- **DON'T** change your plans at the last minute – unless you have

a very good reason.

- **DON'T** tell white lies on order to impress her.

- **DON'T** comment on other women's appearance.

- **DON'T** make promises you can't keep, no matter how small.

man around if he fails to show loads of attention and admiration.

Signs you're in - or not

A Scorpio woman knows exactly how to seduce a man. It's not just her outfit – although it will probably be feminine, seductive and even a little provocative – but rather her eyes, voice and the way she carries herself that makes men pay the most attention. She will smile, flirt, tease and charm you and capture your interest – only to turn around and casually start flirting with someone else. If you're hooked, you'll find yourself striving to hold onto her attention – and that's exactly what she wants: men fighting for her. However, if she really likes you, she won't risk losing you. Her playful interest in other men is merely an effort to sharpen your appetite for her. Unsure about whether her interest is genuine? Look out for the following:

Chances are she will...

- be available when you call
- cancel dates with friends to be with you
- act seductive and take the initiative to be intimate
- be protective towards you ... and fend off other women
- ask what you're up to, casually making sure there's no competition
- make an effort to please you: preparing food, giving you a massage, etc.

Not your type? Making an exit

When a Scorpio woman gives into love, she gives in completely. There is no such thing as 50% commitment in her world – and that applies to romance. She will bond with her man on a very deep level, and when that happens, this flirtatious woman transforms into an incredibly loyal and supportive partner. She will admire him in public, compliment his masculinity and make herself attractive to him in every way. If things are going well, the female Scorpio will make her man the focal point of her life.

If she has really bonded with her partner, she will try her best to make things work – even if that means adjusting her ways. But there are limits to everything, even for a Scorpio in love. If she's not ready to leave, things will get stormy. Eventually, she'll probably give you a verbal black eye, break a few plates, gather her things and slam the door behind her.

Foolproof exit measures:

Remember, she feels passionately about everything. Don't go ahead with these steps unless you are prepared for some emotional blowback.

- Tell her to dress more appropriately and stop looking so cheap
- Never discuss anything with her. You're going to do things your way, and that's it
- Prioritise TV and burgers instead of going to the gym
- Tell her to slow down in bed
- Flirt with other women at the grocery store, the restaurant, the bar, the library...
- Question all of her suggestions and argue whenever possible.

CHAPTER 3

SEX'N STUFF

Seductive moves:
How to get her in the mood:

Sexual chemistry is very important. A Scorpio woman can immediately sense when a man is interested in her, and this spark will soon develop into a burning sexual desire. Miss Scorpio responds well to a man who can say everything she wants to hear by staring into her eyes and whispering erotic suggestions into her ear.

Preferences and erotic nature

Sex is very important to her, and she expects quite a bit from her lover. For one thing, he must display his passionate and sensual sides with ease and confidence. She enjoys getting sexual hints, no matter how small. Don't wait until the two of you are in the bedroom. An erotic encounter with a female Scorpio usually starts several hours before you end up together in bed. Keep this in mind when you're out having dinner. Enjoy your food slowly and seductively and touch her leg with your foot – in other words, communicate with your body language that you're dying to rip her clothes off.

Hitting the right buttons

Although every sign has areas on the body that are more sensitive than others, individual sensitivity may vary quite a bit. Don't go body-blind. Honing in on these erogenous zones and forgetting the rest of her is not a good idea. Use these areas to create sparks while turning her on, and as a passion-booster when things get heated. Watch her body language – including the most obvious of signs. Open your mind to the sensuality of touch and taste.

Key areas
Her private parts

Get it on
Although she has an erotic nature, she doesn't like guys who are blunt and obvious about their advances. But don't worry – there are ways to stimulate her without offending her.

Arouse her
Gently press your body and pelvic area against her when standing in a queue. Arrange her napkin on her lap while having dinner and let your hand linger. If the mood is right and you've sparked her erotic interest, it won't take much friction to turn her on.

Surprise her

You can surprise her by slight modifications to your attitude. Allow your glance to linger a little longer, brush your fingers over her arm and smile seductively. Hold onto the intensity. She will play along as soon as she has picked up on the erotic vibes – and it won't take long.

Spice it up

Add a hint of something forbidden, like a public place (a slight erotic touch when no one is looking, perhaps). Another option might be to arouse her during working hours with a seductive phone call.

Remember: She's not into quickies – to her, they're like grabbing some fast food instead of enjoying a gourmet meal. In other words: if you're in a hurry, don't suggest having sex.

Her expectations

Whispers. Excite her mind. Not familiar with the magic of whispering sensual suggestions into your partner's ear? Start practicing. She is turned on by 'verbal erotics' and the seductive sound of her partner's voice. Sex, to her, is far more than a physical action. Erotic sensations excite her mind as well as her body.

Turn it around. She enjoys experimenting with positions, sexual gadgets – you name it, she'll try it – or at least consider trying it...

Fast mover. When she wants you, she wants you now. Be prepared for sexual action when you least expect it. And keep in mind that she doesn't handle rejection well...

Intense. She has an incredible ability to prolong intercourse by holding back her climax, which can often drive her partner into an intense state of passion.

Bring out the masculinity. Her dream partner is masculine, intense and passionate. He must be erotically adventurous, attentive to her needs and possess a lot of patience and endurance.

Your sensual preferences
Quiz yourself and find out whether this woman is for you.

Where on the scale are you?
1 = Don't agree | 3 = Sure | 5 = Agree!

1. The build-up to sex may start several hours before getting physically intimate.
One a scale for 1 to 5, you are: 1 - 2 - 3- 4 - 5

2. It's impossible to stimulate the body without stimulating the mind.
One a scale for 1 to 5, you are: 1 - 2 - 3- 4 - 5

3. Being expressive and vocal in bed can increase erotic sensations.
One a scale for 1 to 5, you are: 1 - 2 - 3- 4 - 5

4. Quick sex can never replace passionate sensuality.
One a scale for 1 to 5, you are: 1 - 2 - 3- 4 - 5

Score.
15 - 20: You likely share strong sexual chemistry and a fundamental desire for passion and erotic adventures. Enjoy!
14–10: This relationship is sure to include exciting sex – and many opportunities for you to display your passionate side.
9 – 5: You can either give up and get run over, or give in and open your mind to a new world of passionate pleasures.
4–1: This woman may take sex a little more seriously than you do. When she makes love, she gives herself over completely to her partner. Allow yourself to fully experience her.

CHAPTER 4

GENERAL STUFF

The big picture

Keep in mind that the characteristics of a Scorpio may vary quite a bit depending on where within the sign she was born, as well as a wide range of additional astrological factors. But for now, let's stick to the basics. Just remember: don't jump to conclusions as soon as you meet her. Give her room to shine. Get to know the woman behind the sign.

Her personality: Pros and cons

Pros
- Sensual
- Independent
- Passionate
- Committed
- Choosy
- Confident
- Has a strong personality
- A perfectionist
- Sensitive
- Attractive
- Cool and mysterious
- Intelligent
- Compassionate
- Intuitive

Cons
- Jealous
- Reserved
- Suspicious
- Temperamental
- Emotional
- Stubborn
- Sarcastic when provoked
- Seldom forgives and forgets
- Rigid in her views
- Weary of losing control
- Has tunnel vision
- Vengeful
- Demanding
- Calculating

Tip: How to show romantic interest

Try an old-fashioned approach. Call her, invite her out and bring her a little gift – but don't overdo it. Allow her to be intrigued and fascinated by you.

Romantic Vibes

Miss Scorpio:
The intense and committed partner

The essence

Strong feelings. The Scorpio woman feels everything intensely. Either she's in love, or she's not. When a man captures her heart, she'll be completely absorbed by him.

High expectations. She expects a lot of attention from her man. This is why her romances either yield intense relationships – or fail completely. A man who can't handle her intensity will be off pretty quickly.

Don't smooth it over. She doesn't respond well to emotional bribery. After a fight, an attempt to smooth things over with a gift or bunch of flowers will only make matters worse. Instead, he should tell her he's sorry – and why. He needs to let her know that he's aware he messed up and is prepared to do something about it.

100% committed. When a Scorpio woman commits to a man, the relationship engulfs her life. Friends may begin to hear from her less.

Royal treatment. She is very loyal and will pamper, support and show admiration for her partner, both privately and in public – just as long as he doesn't start glancing at other women...! Beware a jealous woman's fury.

Tip: How to show erotic interest

She is intuitive and picks up on hints very quickly. A surprising phone call to ask how she's doing – using a warm and sensual voice – will be enough to convey your message...

Erotic Vibrations

Miss Scorpio:
The passionate and hot lover

The essence

No quickies. Never build her anticipation for sex without delivering. And don't try to wiggle your way out of it by suggesting a quick one. If you've only just met, she'll probably ditch you and look for a more passionate guy.

The **seductress.** When she's made up her mind about seducing a man, she rarely fails. It takes significant self-control to resist her voice and hypnotic eyes.

Don't put on a show. There's nothing casual about her sex life. To her, having sex means giving 100%. If not, you might as well be watching TV.

Bring out the passion! She is a demanding lover with loads of energy and endurance. She will take it as a personal insult if you turn your back on her after only 15 minutes of intense lovemaking.

Erotic wavelength. If you manage to establish a strong sensual chemistry with her, she will treat you like a king and pamper you in every possible way, not only sexually.

CHAPTER 5

COMPATIBILITY QUIZ

Are you banging your head against the wall, or does she unleash your positive potential? Do you provoke her or bring out the best in her? Is she making you throw your arms into the air in exasperation, or do you feel inspired and complete in her company? Take the test to find out.

Question no 1
You are having a wonderful time at a party and feeling great. What would you do if your girlfriend accused you of flirting with other women?

A – That would never happen because I would never do anything to make her feel insecure. I'm friendly with both men and women, but I never flirt.
B – Just typical! I might as well sit down in a corner and sulk.
C – I would put my arms around her and use my body language to reassure her that although many women are there, she is the woman.

Question no 2
What kind of woman do you prefer? Someone who's open, frank and straight to the point, or someone who's slightly mysterious?

A – I'm no mind reader. I like women who won't leave me guessing.
B – A little bit of both, really. It depends on the woman.
C – I love mysterious women. They are like treasure chests, waiting to be discovered and explored.

(cont.)

Question no 3
Have you ever been tempted to test a woman's love for you by flirting with others?

A – Of course. It's the only way to find out how she feels about me.
B – No, never. If I care about her, why would I want to make her feel jealous?
C – Sometimes, but only for fun – never anything serious.

Question no 4
How do you respond when your partner decides to change your erotic routine and introduce something new?

A - Great! I'd love that.
B - I wouldn't like that. I prefer the quiet comforts of sex.
C – It'd be fine, provided it gives us both pleasure.

Question no 5
Would you consider yourself mentally strong?

A – Yo, stupid question! I'm one of the strongest guys at the gym!
B – Yes, although we all have our ups and downs. Generally, I'm not easily pushed off balance.
C – I've never really thought about it. About average, I guess.

Question no 6
Would you keep in touch with your female friends after starting a new relationship?

A – No, that would feel a bit awkward.
B – Yes, but on a different level – and not often. I would always be open about it, too.
C - Yes! I like women, and I don't want to lose friends just for the sake of a relationship. I would also stay in touch with ex-girlfriends.

Question no 7
Do you often find yourself in heated debates?

A – Yes, I have strong opinions about most things.
B – No. I'm not easily provoked.
C – Not often, but sometimes – only if the topic is important to me.

Question no 8
You have planned to go out with the guys. How would you respond if your girlfriend looked at you seductively and said, 'I thought we might have some alone time tonight?'

A - She sometimes does that, but I don't care. I'd go out with the guys anyway.
B – Hmm ... this is a difficult one. It would depend on what we'd had planned.
C - I would probably cancel on the guys. She can be very seductive and persuasive.

Question no 9
Have you ever turned a woman on without seeing it through?

A – No, never. I'd hate it if she did that to me.
B - Sure, I'm a handsome guy. Plus, she's easily aroused, and I can't be expected to deliver 24/7.
C - Very seldom, and only if I've been in a hurry, or we've been out in public or something like that.

Question no 10
Do you think it's okay to have a fling with a stranger when you're dating another woman?

A - No problem. Life is for living, and I've got a great appetite for sex.
B - It depends on who committed to the woman.
C – Nope! Never!

SCORE	A	B	C
Question 1	10	1	5
Question 2	1	5	10
Question 3	1	10	5
Question 4	5	1	10
Question 5	1	10	5
Question 6	10	5	1
Question 7	5	10	1
Question 8	1	5	10
Question 9	10	1	5
Question 10	1	5	10

75 – 100

You have either cheated during the quiz to get optimal answers – or else entered one of the most rewarding, exciting, loving, passionate and sexiest relationships out there. You can communicate without uttering a single word – sometimes even a glance and a smile is enough. She is sharp, independent, loyal and passionate, and she manages to bring out the fire on you – on many levels. You respect and admire each other. Everything feels right. The base for this relationship is strong. Enjoy it.

51 – 74

Loads of fun. Loads of sex. Loads of passion and excitement. You have captured a woman who is energetic and demanding, and you know exactly how to handle her. Boredom will never be a problem for you two. You share her enthusiasm for keeping life interesting, so it's no wonder that every day seems like a new adventure. You may experience a fight from time to time, but don't be put off. The female Scorpio will apologise when she realises that she has done you wrong – even if it takes her weeks or months to admit it. Keep in mind that this woman needs to be on her own every now and then. Don't take it personally; it's got nothing to do with you. Let her have her moments of solitude, and she'll return to you as soon as she's recharged her mental battery.

26 – 50

What made you enter into a relationship with her? Her body and passionate sensuality? Either you're a very patient guy, or you have come across a rare flexible Scorpio. It's time to figure out what you're looking for in a woman and what makes you happy – as well as whether you have what makes her happy. The female Scorpio needs support from a caring partner. This means a few things for you: try to ignore her fierce temper. Don't always try to persuade her that you're right. Don't be too independent – but don't be too dependent, either. Respond with humour when you want to respond with anger. Support her, even when you're tempted to throw your hands in the air. Who knows, she may turn out to be the woman after all.

10 – 25

The magic has disappeared like the morning dew from a flower. She is probably not the woman you thought she was. It doesn't matter that she makes you feel like a king in bed if the bliss disappears as soon as the alarm clock goes off. You're disconnected on many levels, and her expectations and values are different to yours. The constant tension will begin to wear you out after a while. Do you regularly misunderstand each other? Communicate. If the disagreements are non-negotiable, then it might be best to hunt for happiness elsewhere.

Thoughts...
Don't make assumptions. Make sure you are moving in the same direction. Not sure where you are going? Ask her.

...just a final note:
This book has not been approved by your date and should be treated accordingly. He or she *may* not agree with the content.

www.ingramcontent.com/pod-product-compliance
Lightning Source LLC
Chambersburg PA
CBHW060039040426
42331CB00032B/1785